GOOD MANNERS on the PHONE

The Child's World

Published by The Child's World®
1980 Lookout Drive • Mankato, MN 56003-1705
800-599-READ • www.childsworld.com

Acknowledgments
The Child's World®: Mary Berendes, Publishing Director
The Design Lab: Design and production
Red Line Editorial: Editorial direction

ISBN 9781614732280
LCCN 2012932471

Printed in the United States of America
Mankato, MN
July 2012
PA02126

ABOUT THE AUTHOR

Ann Ingalls writes stories and poems for people of all ages as well as resource materials for parents and teachers. She was a teacher for many years and enjoys working with children. When she isn't writing, she enjoys spending time with her family and friends, traveling, reading, knitting, and playing with her cats.

ABOUT THE ILLUSTRATOR

Ronnie Rooney took art classes constantly as a child. She was always drawing and painting at her mom's kitchen table. She got her BFA in painting from the University of Massachusetts at Amherst and her MFA in Illustration from Savannah College of Art and Design in Savannah, Georgia. She now lives and works in Fort Lewis, Washington. Her plan is to pass her love of art and sports on to her two young children.

CONTENTS

Manners on the Phone

Do you want to have friends? Do you want to be **welcome** wherever you go? The best way to do this is to learn good manners. You learn them by watching the way people treat one another. Think about how you like others to treat you. You can learn good manners from your family, your teachers, and adults who care for you.

One of the many places to use good manners is on the telephone. It is just as important to be **polite** when talking on the phone as it is when talking to others in person.

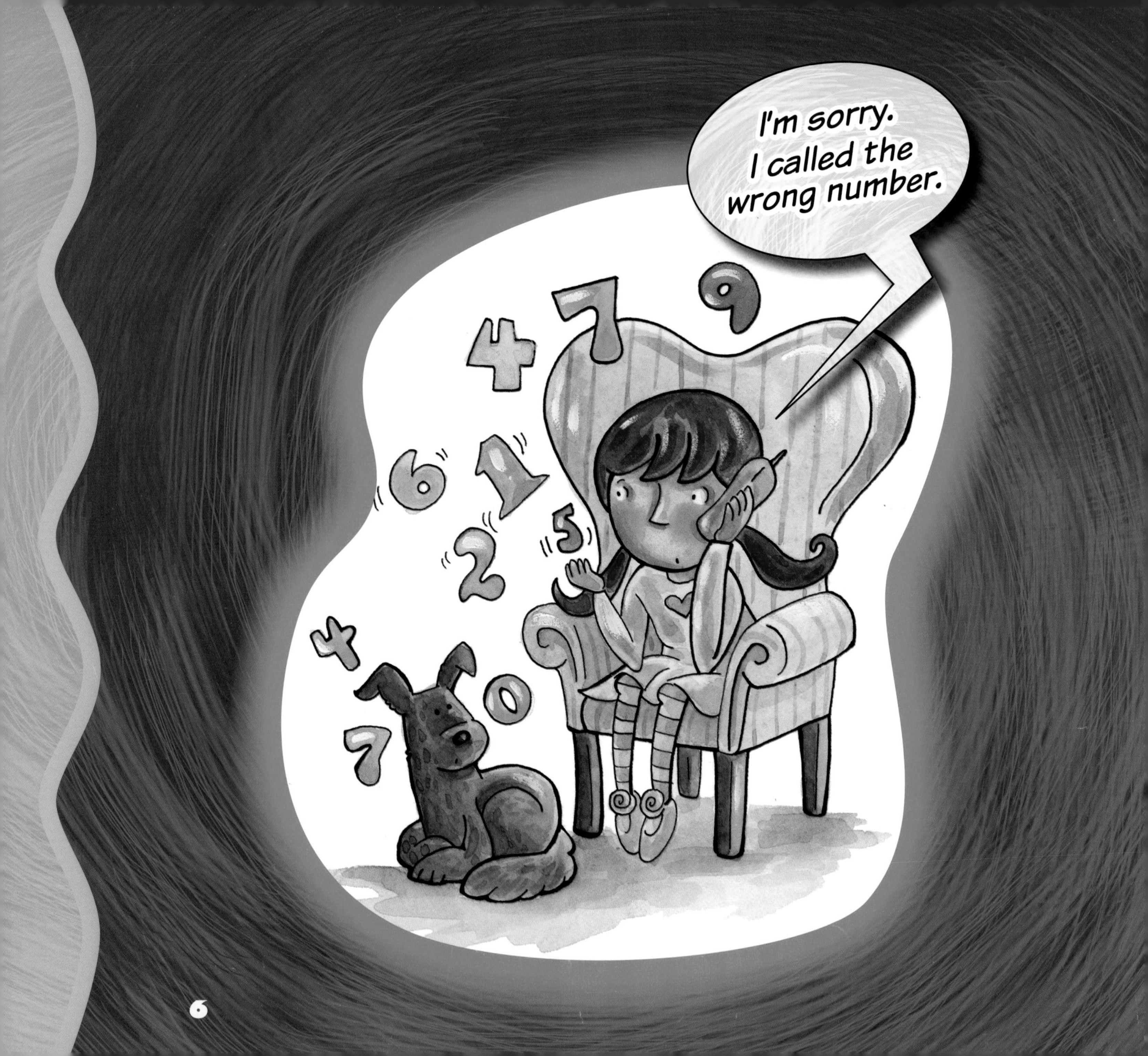
I'm sorry. I called the wrong number.

Before You Dial

Make sure you have the right phone number. This way you do not bother strangers. If you do **dial** a wrong number, say "I'm sorry. I called the wrong number." Then hang up.

Know the name or title of the person with whom you want to speak. And have a good idea of what you would like to talk about.

Have a notepad and pen handy. If you get important **information** during the call, you can write it down.

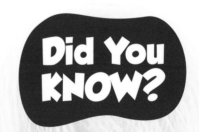

Did You KNOW?

The first telephone was made about 125 years ago. It was invented by Alexander Graham Bell.

When to Call

Do not call people early in the morning or late at night.
They may be sleeping.

Try not to call when people are eating their meals.
So no calls before 8 a.m. No calls at lunch around noon.
And dinner is around 6 p.m. to 7 p.m. Who knows? The
person you call may be holding a sticky chicken leg.

Keep your call short. The person you are calling might
be busy. She could be juggling rings or taming lions. If you
know someone is busy at a certain time, call later.

What to Say When You Call

When you make a phone call, give your name. Do not pretend to be the queen of England. Then you can ask for the person you are calling.

Enjoy your **conversation**! Do not shout. Do not grunt. Do not roar. Speak clearly in a friendly voice.

Don't forget to say "goodbye" when you are done talking. If you are talking to a friend or family member, you could say "Toodles," "Hasta luego," "See you later, alligator," or "Bye-bye, pumpkin pie."

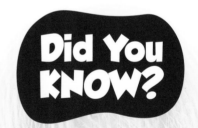

Did You KNOW?

China has more phones than any other country. There are about 314 million phones in China.

Answering the Phone

Good manners are just as important when someone calls you. When you hear the telephone ring, pick it up as quickly as you can. The best way to answer a telephone is to say "Hello," not "Okey-dokey" or "What do you want?"

If the caller wants to talk with you, say "This is Anna." You can also say, "Anna speaking."

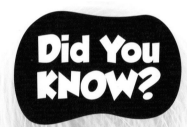

Did You KNOW?

In Italy, you say "Pronto!" when you answer the phone.

What to Say When You Answer a Call

If the caller wants to talk to someone else, say, "Just a moment, please." Then set down the phone gently while you get that person. Do not slam the phone down. *Blam!* The person at the other end may still have the phone close to her ear. A quick, sharp bang can hurt and it is rude. You would not like that if someone did that to you. Don't yell for that person while you're holding the phone close by. You could be yelling into the caller's ear!

Taking a Message

The person who is wanted on the phone may be busy or not at home. You will need to take a message. You do not need to tell the caller what the person is doing. It is not a good idea for you to say, "My mother is in the tub right now. She is soaking wet." But you could say, "My mother is busy. May I take a message?" If your brother is at football practice, take a message. Say, "He cannot come to the phone right now. He will call you back later."

Be sure to write down the name of the caller. And write down the caller's phone number, too. Use your very best printing.

Is the Caller a Stranger?

If caller wants to speak to someone who is not home, say, "Who is calling? She will call you back soon." Never tell a caller that no adults are home. If the caller asks, "Where is she?" repeat, "My mother is busy. May I take a message?"

Who is calling?

If the caller asks for your name, just give him your last name. You might say, "This is the Jones family." Do not answer questions like "Who are you?" or "What is your name?" or "Where do you live?" Just say, "Who is calling, please?" Never give any other information.

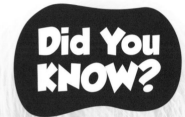

Did You KNOW?

You can call 9-1-1 anywhere in the United States if there is an emergency. Other countries have other emergency numbers. You should NEVER call 9-1-1 unless there is a real emergency. Someone else may really need help.

A Bit More Polite

With cell phones, we are able to make and take calls from almost anywhere. A few more tips will keep your calls at their very best!

- Be **discreet** when you eat. A phone call is not the time to chomp, chew, or snack. Would you want to listen to someone slurping soup into your ear?

- Try to find a quiet place for your call. Talking to your dad while you watch TV and play your stereo during your vacuuming time does not show him that you are listening to him.

- Do not use the phone while you're using the bathroom. Gross!

• Be safe and help your grown-ups stay smart. Using a cell phone while driving is never a good idea.

It is a good idea to practice using the phone. Pretend to be a caller. Pretend to answer the phone. With a little practice, you'll be ready to dial in style!

Quick QUIZ

Put your new phone manners in action with this pop quiz! Will you make the right call?

The best time to call someone is when:
a. you think they are in the bathtub.
b. you know they are asleep.
c. you think they are not busy.
d. you know they are standing on a roof.

When you call someone, be sure:
a. to use a scary voice.
b. to use your normal voice.
c. to sing a song.
d. to use a squeaky voice.

When you pick up the phone, be sure to say:
a. "This is Pete's Pizza Parlor."
b. "No one is home right now."
c. "Sorry, you have got the wrong number." Say this even if the caller has the right number.
d. "Hello." Then tell your name.

Check the number before you call if:
a. you want to speak to the right person.
b. you want to bother strangers.
c. you want to wake someone up.
d. you want to bother someone when they are eating.

If you take a phone message, be sure to:

a. write the name and number down later.
b. write the name and number down right away.
c. write the name and number on a scrap of paper. Then throw it away.
d. write the name and number in ketchup on a piece of bread.

If you call the wrong number say:

a. "Too bad, so sad."
b. "Can you talk to me anyway?"
c. "I am sorry. I have the wrong number."
d. "Are you sure?"

When you hang up the phone, it is best to do it:

a. gently.
b. with a big bang.
c. by dropping it on the floor.
d. by throwing it in the trash.

Glossary

conversation (kon-vur-SAY-shuhn): If you have a conversation, you talk with someone for a while. Be polite during your phone conversation.

dial (DIE-uhl): To dial is to enter telephone numbers into a phone by pressing buttons. Make sure you dial the right phone number.

discreet (diss-KREET): If you are discreet, you know the right thing to say and can be trusted to keep secrets. Be discreet when talking on the phone with a stranger.

emergency (i-MUR-juhn-see): An emergency is a sudden and dangerous event that needs to be quickly fixed. In an emergency, you should dial 9-1-1.

information (in-fur-MAY-shuhn): Information is facts and what you learn and know. Some information should not be told to others on the phone.

polite (puh-LITE): To be polite is to have good manners. It is important to be polite on the phone.

welcome (WEL-kuhm): People are welcome when a host feels glad to have them in his or her home. Mary feels welcome at Karen's house.

Books

Burstein, John. *Manners, Please!: Why It Pays to be Polite*. New York: Crabtree, 2011.

Eberly, Sheryl. *365 Manners Kids Should Know: Games, Activities, and Other Fun Ways to Help Children Learn Etiquette*. New York: Three Rivers Press, 2001.

Espeland, Pamela. *Dude, That's Rude!* Minneapolis, MN: Free Spirit Publishing, 2007.

Web Sites

Visit our Web site for links about manners on the phone: **childsworld.com/links**

Note to Parents, Teachers, and Librarians: We routinely verify our Web links to make sure they are safe and active sites. So encourage your readers to check them out!

Index